Beale Street

and Other Classic Blues

38 Works, 1901–1921

Edited by

DAVID A. JASEN

DOVER PUBLICATIONS, INC.
Mineola, New York

DOVER MUSICAL ARCHIVES

PUBLISHER'S NOTE

Since the originals reproduced here are faithful historical documents as well as sources of enjoyment, the titles and artwork have not been changed even where they reflect the broader humor of their era, in which the nation was far less sensitive to jibes about minority groups. It is our belief that a mature understanding of our past is more fruitful than a falsification of history.

Bibliographical Note

Beale Street and Other Classic Blues: 38 Works, 1901–1921 is a new collection of music, selected and with an introduction by David A. Jasen, first published by Dover Publications, Inc., in 1998. The original publishers and dates of publication of the music appear in the Contents and on the individual covers and title pages.

International Standard Book Number: 0-486-40183-9

Manufactured in the United States of America
Dover Publications, Inc., 31 East 2nd Street, Mineola, N.Y. 11501

INTRODUCTION

When asked in court to describe the blues, the expert witness replied, "Blues is *blues,* your Honor."

That definition suggests that one ought to know the blues when one hears it—that wonderfully lucid 12-bar form with its satisfyingly simple, inevitable, self-enclosing harmonic functions. "Now, *that's* the blues," we might say—and we'd be right.

But the tag "blues" is far from confined to that form we think of as authentic. Regularly published from 1912, "blues" pieces of all sorts were fair game for every commercial publisher as the tag was affixed to ragtime and pop tunes, piano solos and syncopated songs—virtually anything that even hinted at the tell-tale "blue notes"—the flatted 3rd, flatted 5th and flatted 7th—of the major scale. (Play an unadorned C major scale, then sprinkle it lightly with E-flats, G-flats and B-flats. *Voilà!* Instant blues!)

By 1921, a great variety of music was labelled "blues" as the concept became still more inclusive. This folio celebrates the best of those songs and instrumentals—for great, near-great and merely wonderful pieces have the character to survive, no matter *what* we call them!

●

William Christopher Handy (1873–1958), while not quite the "Father of the Blues," was surely its most important proselytizer—writing about the form, publishing works by other composers and lyricists, and producing thirteen of his own blues between 1912 ("The Memphis Blues") and 1921 ("Aunt Hagar's Children Blues"). His "The Saint Louis Blues" (1914) became the first million-selling blues—the most recorded song in Tin Pan Alley history until the onset of the rock-'n'-roll era—and the first song to have a short film made of it (starring legendary singer Bessie Smith). Handy was among the first to have entire recorded albums devoted to his music. He edited the first book on the blues—his *Blues: An Anthology* (1926)—talking at length about its origin and his first encounter with that music. His autobiography, *Father of the Blues* (1941), led to a film biography called *St. Louis Blues* (1957), with Nat "King" Cole portraying Handy. The United States Postal Service honored him with a stamp; and, in Memphis, Tennessee, his statue graces the town park.

Composer-publisher Perry Bradford (1893–1970) opened the recording field to singers of the blues when he obtained a record contract for Mamie Smith—the first black woman to record the blues. Backed by her Jazz Hounds (pictured on our sheet music cover, p. 9), Smith's 1920 recording of Bradford's "Crazy Blues" started the blues revolution on disks that continues to the present. In 1916, Bradford self-published his first number, "The Lonesome Blues," then sold it to publisher Fred Bowers, who reissued the music two years later. Bradford's blues seems earthier than Handy's, perhaps reflecting the composer's Southern heritage and vaudeville training.

Publishing in hometown New Orleans, then in Chicago, Clarence Williams (1893–1965) issued over four hundred songs, taking credit in more than half of them as composer, co-composer or lyricist. In 1919, he teamed up with Spencer Williams (they were not related) for "Royal Garden Blues," his first big hit. The song's 1921 recording by the Original Dixieland Jazz Band made it a great favorite with other Dixieland groups, leading to its eventual status as a blues standard. Williams' "Sugar Blues," also issued in 1919, became a standard as well thanks to its million-selling muted-trumpet recording by Clyde McCoy in 1935. In 1921, Williams edged the blues away from Handy's and Bradford's domination when he moved his operations to New York City, joining the very competitive, very lucrative battle-of-the-blues.

Chris Smith (1879–1949) was a marvelous black songwriter with such hits as "I've Got De Blues" (the earliest song with "blues" in its title, written with lyricist Elmer Bowman, 1901), "San Francisco Blues" (an early blues instrumental, 1916), and "The Farm Yard Blues" (1917). (On our page 17, that's Smith at the keyboard and singer-collaborator Henry Troy perched above.) A long-time contributor to the songbags of both black and white performers, and of interpolated hit songs in Broadway shows, Smith joined W. C. Handy in 1920 as lyricist for "Long Gone."

The first jazz record, "Livery Stable Blues," was made by the Original Dixieland Jazz Band on February 26, 1917, copyrighted not by the ODJB but by trumpeter Ray Lopez and Alcide Nunez, the group's former clarinetist. Another jazz standard originally made famous by the band was Tom Delaney's "The Jazz-Me Blues." Anything *but* a blues, it was and remains one of the great snappy, syncopated jazz tunes firmly entrenched in the jazz-band repertoire. Delaney (dates unknown) is also represented in our collection by "The Down Home Blues" (1921), a very satisfying blues number.

Three great ragtime composer-pianists share their music with us as well. Artie Matthews (1888–1958)—known for his five "Pastime Rags"—composed his perennial favorite "The Weary Blues" in 1915. Ferdinand "Jelly Roll" Morton (1890–1941), a legendary ragtimer and jazz composer-pianist, issued his "The Jelly Roll Blues" in 1915, when he was in Chicago. Luckeyth ("Lucky") Roberts (1887–1968) made a piano roll of "Railroad Blues," which picked up steam when the Benson Orchestra made its hit recording on September 21, 1920.

•

A wide variety of blues, to be sure! But that very range of musical tastes and commercial tags represents an American phenomenon in all its depth and rich confusion, reflecting the spirit of a certain time. Publishers fulfilled their needs then as now, and the music-loving public—ready as ever for a great tune, a catchy beat, or a memorable turn-of-phrase—made "standards" and "classics" of the best of the lot . . . or of the ones that simply appealed to their fancy of the moment. Unique in our musical history—and still wonderful to play and hear—these are indeed our classic blues.

David A. Jasen

CONTENTS

AUNT HAGAR'S CHILDREN BLUES

BY W. C. HANDY

PUBLISHED BY
HANDY BROS.
MUSIC CO. INC.
SUCCESSORS TO PACE & HANDY MUSIC CO. INC.
(HOME OF THE BLUES)
232 W. 46th ST. NEW YORK CITY

ORIGINATOR OF THE BLUES

STADMER

Aunt Hagar's Children Blues

Adaptation from W. C. Handy's Selection
"Aunt Hagar's Children"

Lyrics by
Lieut. J. TIM BRYMM

Music by
W. C. HANDY

Old Dea-con Spliv-ins, his flock was giv-in' The way of liv-in' right, Said he no wing-ing, no rag-time sing-ing here to-night _____ Up jump - ed Aunt Ha-

2

Chorus

Hear Aunt Ha-gar's child-ren har-mon-iz-ing, Hear that sweet mel - o - dy It's

like a choir— from on high broke loose —————————— If the

dev - il brought it, the good Lord sent it right down to me. I—

don't know what it's called but be-lieve me It is one mourn-ful blues. blues.

Patter

Um! 'taint no use in talk-in' Um! Ha-gar's chil-dren squawk-in'

Such jazz-a-pa-tion, such mod-u-la-tion When my feet say dance I

just can't re-fuse— When I hear— that mel-o-dy they call the

Blues Aunt Ha-gar's chil dren Blues Some Blues, Some Blues.

BEALE STREET

ANOTHER MEMPHIS "BLUES"
BY
W. C. HANDY

Published by PACE & HANDY MUSIC CO. Memphis, Tenn.

— 5 —

"HOME OF THE BLUES"

BEALE STREET

Respectfully dedicated to Sam and Nello Pacini.

Words & Music
by W.C.HANDY.

I've seen the lights of gay Broad-
The sev-en won-ders of the world I've

way,____
seen____

Old Mar-ket Street down by the Fris-co Bay,____
And ma-ny are the plac-es I have been.____

____ I've strolled the Pra-do, I've gambled on the Bourse____
____ Take my ad-vice folks and see Beale Street first.____

You'll see pret-ty Browns in beau-ti-ful gowns,You'll see tail-or mades and
You'll see Hog-Nose res-trants and Chit-lin' Ca-fes You'll see Jugs that tell of
You'll see men who rank with the first in the nation Who come to Beale for
If Beale Street could talk If Beale Street could talk, Mar-ried men would have to take their

hand me, downs You'll meet hon-est men and pick-pock-ets skilled You'll find that
by - gone days And pla - ces, once pla - ces, now just a sham, You'll see
in - spi - ra - tion. Pol - i - ti - cians call you a dub Un - less you've
beds and walk Ex - cept one or two, who nev - er drank booze And the

bus' - ness nev - er clos - es till some - bod - y gets killed.
Gold - en Balls e - nough to pave the New Je - ru - sa - lem.
been in - i - ti - a - ted in the Rick - ri - ters Club.
blind man on the cor - ner who sings the Beale Street Blues.

BEALE STREET BLUES

I'd rath-er be here, than an - y place I know, I'd rath-er
Goin' to the ri - ver, may - be, bye and bye Goin' to the

be here than an - y place I know It's goin' to
ri - ver, and there's a rea - son why Be - cause the

take the Ser - gent For to make me go,
ri - vers wet And Beale Streets done gone dry.

CRAZY BLUES

By PERRY BRADFORD

MAMIE SMITH AND HER JAZZ HOUNDS

Get this number for your phonograph on Okeh Record No. 4169

Published by

PERRY BRADFORD

MUSIC PUB. CO.

1547 Broadway, N. Y. C.

CRAZY BLUES

By PERRY BRADFORD

I can't_ sleep at
I am_ feel - in'

night   I can't_ eat a bite   'Cause the one I love
sad   Noth-ing_ makes me glad   Since my babe went a-way

He don't treat_ me right   It makes me feel so blue
Near-ly drives_ me mad   It makes me feel so bad

I don't know what to do   Some-times I sit and sigh   And then be-gan to cry
And I'm so ver-y sore   Some-time I cry and moan   He left me all a-lone

He went a-way___ and nev-er said good-bye_____ I could
He went a-way___ and left me all___ a - lone_____ Went down

read his let-ters but I sure can't read his mind_____
to the rail-road and laid my head on the track_____

I tho't he's lov-ing me and he was leav-ing all the time_____
I tho't a-bout ba-by and then I quick-ly snatched it back_____

So now I've seen___ that my poor love was blind_____ So
My ba - by gone___ and he gave me the sack_____

The Down Home Blues

Words and Music
by
TOM DELANEY

PUBLISHED BY
Albury & Delaney Music Pub. Co.
257 W. 138th STR., NEW YORK CITY

Successfully featured by
ETHEL WATERS
ON BLACK SWAN RECORD
No. 2010

The Down Home Blues

Words and Music
by TOM DELANEY

Chorus

Woke up this morn - in'   the day was dawnin'   And I was feel-in' all
No use in greiv - in'   Be-cause I'm leavin'   I'm bro-ken hearted and

sad and blue   I had no-bod - y   to tell my troubles to
Dix - ie bound lawd   I've been mistreat-ed   Aint got no time   to loose

I   felt   so wor-ried   I didn't know what to
My   train   is wait - in'   And I've got the down home

do_____   But there's
blues_____

The Farm Yard Blues
(I Miss My Mississippi Home)

By CHRIS SMITH & HENRY TROY

Moderato — Vamp — VOICE

won-der what's the mat-ter now with me ____ I'm feel-in' just as blue as I can be ____
been most ev-'ry place there is to go ____ I know most ev-'ry-thing there is to know ____

I guess the rea-son why I feel so dip-py, I'm so far a-way from Miss-is-sip-pi;
I've stayed a-while in ev-'ry well-known ci-ty, But I could live and die in Miss-is-sip-pi;

Good-ness knows there ain't no place like home, ____ I miss it in a thou-sand diff-'rent ways, ____ I've got the
Ev-'ry-bo-dy tells you "How de do?" ____ I'm fond of southern hos-pi-tal-i-ty, ____ No matter

farm-yard blues, I long for barn-yard news, For it seems I've been a-way a mil-lion days. ____
where you am; Just so is Dix-ie-land, You ____ simp-ly have to say the same as me. ____

"THE HESITATING BLUES"

Words & Music by
W. C. HANDY

wait? Please give me 2 9 8,__ Why do you hes - i -
wait? Come be my wife my Kate, Why do you hes - i -

tate? _____ What you say, can't
tate?" _____ I -de - clined him

talk to my Brown! A storm last night blowed the wires all down; Tell me
just for a stall— He left__ that night on the Can - non Ball; Hon-ey,

how long will__ I have to wait?
how long will__ I have to wait?

Oh, won't you tell me now — Why do you hes - i - tate?
Will he come back now — Or will he hes - i - tate?

CHORUS

"Pro-cras-ti - na - tion is the thief of time," So all the wise owls

say, _____ "One stitch in time may save nine,"

To-morrow's not to - day. And if you put off

Somebody's bound to lose. I'd be his,

he'd be mine, And I'd be feel-ing gay, Left a lone

to grieve and pine, My best friend's gone a - way, He's gone and

left me The Hes - i -tat -ing Blues.

D.S.

The Hindenburg Blues.

Arranged by
ETHEL ALCORN.

Words and music by
SANDERS REYNOLDS.

1. Ole mammy
2. Now Sammy

Snow   who's 'bout sev - en - ty fo', Lives way down South in Al-a - bam; She's thinking of   Dis a
Snow will know just ex - actly where to go, When he goes glidin' over No man's land. It won't be far   To the

boy who's gone to   war_____   Well, you nev - er hear her mur-mur not a
Kai - ser's front   door_____   An' when he starts a knock-in', kick-in',

mum - bl - in' word, 'Cause she knows dis lov - in' son will be a - mongst de birds— Dat-ll
bump - in' things 'round, Dey will know dat Un - cle Sam - my's boy's have flew in town— 'Cause dey'll

roost a-round the Kai-ser's bed;_____ An' ev - 'ry mornin', noon an' night, Fo' she knows her boy kin fight, Dis is
soon be number'd' mongst de dead_____

The Hooking Cow Blues

Words & Music by
DOUGLASS WILLIAMS
Jazz & Blues Music by
W. C. HANDY.

Copyright **1917** transferred to Pace & Handy Music Co., Memphis, Tenn.

29

If You Don't Believe I Love You
(Look What A Fool Ive Been)

Words & Music by
CLARENCE WILLIAMS
Writer of "Royal Garden Blues"

I'm wise to you ba - by / Think that I'm goin' a - way___ / Peo - ple call me
You might have been hap - py / If you had on - ly tried___ / Why not tell the

cra - zy / fool - ish for to stay / You've got all my lov - ing
truth dear / 'stead of tell - in' lies / I al - ways be - lieved you

say - ing I'm not true / When you say you don't want me / It makes me feel blue.
but I can't no more / Don't come hanging a - round me / I want you to know.

Chorus

Off my mind you're so un-kind I'm go-ing a-way Yes go-ing a-way to stay——

———— Just be-fore I met you I had a good pair of shoes but take a
———— Keep a-fool-ing with me I'll catch a rail off a fence I'll beat you
———— You were out of a job Your mon-ey sho' was all gone you know that

look at me now— I got the bare-foot-ed blues so
ov-er the head— And I will learn you some sense so If you don't be lieve I
I bust-ed Suds— to get your clothes out of pawn so

love you Look what a fool I've been.—— been.——

I'M CRAZY 'BOUT YOUR LOVIN' AND I WANTS IT ALL THE TIME
WORDS AND MUSIC BY PERRY BRADFORD
5
STARMER
FREDERICK V. BOWERS INC.
BOWERS' SONGS TOUCH THE HEART
MUSIC PUBLISHERS NEW YORK CITY

I'm Crazy 'Bout Your Lovin'
And I Want It All The Time

By PERRY BRADFORD
Writer of "Lonesome Blues" "Stewin de Rice"
What Did Deacon Jones do?

I've got a lov-in dad-dy / Who cert'nly can love
Oh gee! but I am lone-ly / My lov-in' man's gone a-

sweet / When he commence to kiss - in' / He really can't be beat
way / I'm thinking of him on - ly / I miss him night and day

He loves me in the morning he hugs me at night He gives me lots of lov-ing and
Yes, I am so craz-y 'bout him, Yes I must admit With his hon-ey ba-by cer- ten-

treats me just right That lov-in' dad - dy of mine he's so fine.
ly makes a hit That cru-el dad - dy of mine folks he's fine.

I'M FREE, SINGLE, DISENGAGED, LOOKING FOR SOMEONE TO LOVE

Words and Music by
TYUS and TYUS

Originally Introduced
by
MAMIE SMITH

Ted Browne Music Co.
325 MADISON STREET
Chicago

I'm Free, Single, Disengaged, Looking for Someone to Love

Words by
CHARLES TYUS

Music by
EFFIE TYUS

Moderato

Vamp

I can't see how it can be
Some-times I feel sad and blue,

Ev'-ry-bod-y has a sweet-ie but me, No mat-ter
I don't know what in this world to do, Some times I

39

how I try,   I   don't see   why,   It hurts me so, it makes me
lay a - wake   'till the break of   morn,   Re-gret-ting the   day that

sigh and   cry,   Please won't someone come and take a   chance with me,
I   was   born,   I   am just as lone - ly, lone - ly   as   can   be,

Love me   like   a   moth - er would   a   ba - by   on   her   knee.
Want some - one   to   buzz a - round   me   like a   bum - ble   bee.

CHORUS   *p-f* *a tempo*
I'm free,   sing - le,   dis - en - gaged,   Look-ing for some - one   to

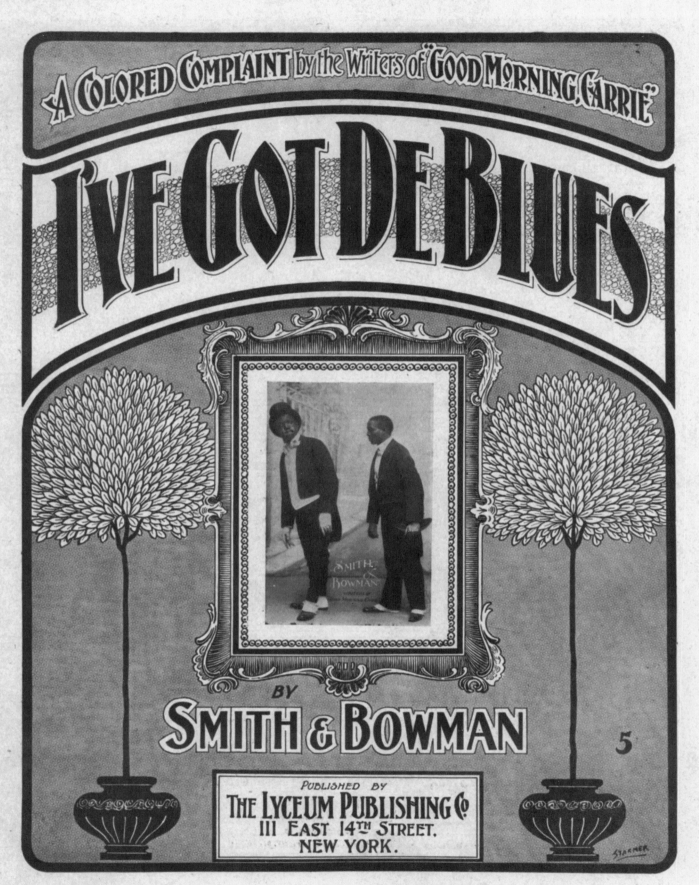

I've got de Blues.

By SMITH & BOWMAN.

1. Big Sam John-son was a pop-u-lar man A-mong Dark-town's é-lite, They made him toast-mas-ter at ev'-ry af-fair,__ 'Cause his speech-es were cert'-ny a treat; He

2. Sam thought he'd take Li-za to a coon show, He start-ed out to walk, He wore a ver-y loud__ suit__ of clothes, It was real-ly quite loud 'nuff to talk; He

took his Li - za to a ban-quet last night, As he rose to speak he
sat a mo - ment on a bench in the park, It had just been paint - ed

poco rit.

spied, His ri - val and his Lize, both a - mak-ing goo goo eyes, Then poor
blue, His blood in an-ger boiled, when he saw his clothes were spoiled, And to

rall.

Sam for - got his toast and sad - ly sighed;_____
moan these words was all that he could do:_____

Chorus. *Slow*

1. I've got de blues, I beg to be__ ex - cused; My
2. I've got de blues, I beg to be__ ex - cused; My

THE JAZZ-ME BLUES

BY
TOM DELANEY

Published by
PALMETTO MUSIC PUB. CO.,
New York

EXCLUSIVE SELLING AGENTS
EDWARD B. MARKS MUSIC CO.
102-104 W. 38th St.,
New York

THE JAZZ ME BLUES

Words and Music by
TOM DELANEY

THE JELLY ROLL BLUES

"The Original Jelly Roll"

FERD. MORTON.

Tempo di Blues

Copyright MCMXV by Will Rossiter, Chicago.

JOE TURNER BLUES

W. C. HANDY

Slowly

You'll nev-er miss the wa-ter   till your well runs
I bought a bull-dog for to   watch you while you
Some-times I feel like noth-in',   some-thin' throwed a-

dry, _____   Till your well runs dry. _____
sleep, _____   Guard you while you sleep. _____
way, _____   Some-thin' throwed a-way. _____

THE JOGO BLUES
PLAYED BY
HANDY AND HIS BANDS
AS THE MEMPHIS ITCH
BY
W. C. HANDY
AUTHOR OF
"THE GIRL YOU NEVER HAVE MET"
RESPECTFULLY
DEDICATED TO
MR. JOHN ROSS
MEMPHIS TENN.
JOGO BLUES
PUBLISHED BY
PACE & HANDY
MUSIC CO
NEW YORK N.Y

THE JOGO BLUES

By W. C. HANDY

Con Spirito

The Kaiser's Got The Blues
He's Got Those Weary Blues
WORDS BY
DOMER C. BROWNE
MUSIC BY
W. C. HANDY
P&H
7
5
PUBLISHED BY
PACE & HANDY
MUSIC CO. INC.
(HOME OF THE BLUES)
GAIETY THEATRE BUILDING
1547 BROADWAY, NEW YORK CITY.
STARMER N.Y.

Respectfully dedicated to Irwin S. Cobb.

The Kaiser's Got The Blues
(He's Got The Weary Blues)

Words & Music by
DOMER C BROWNE
& W C HANDY

Chorus.

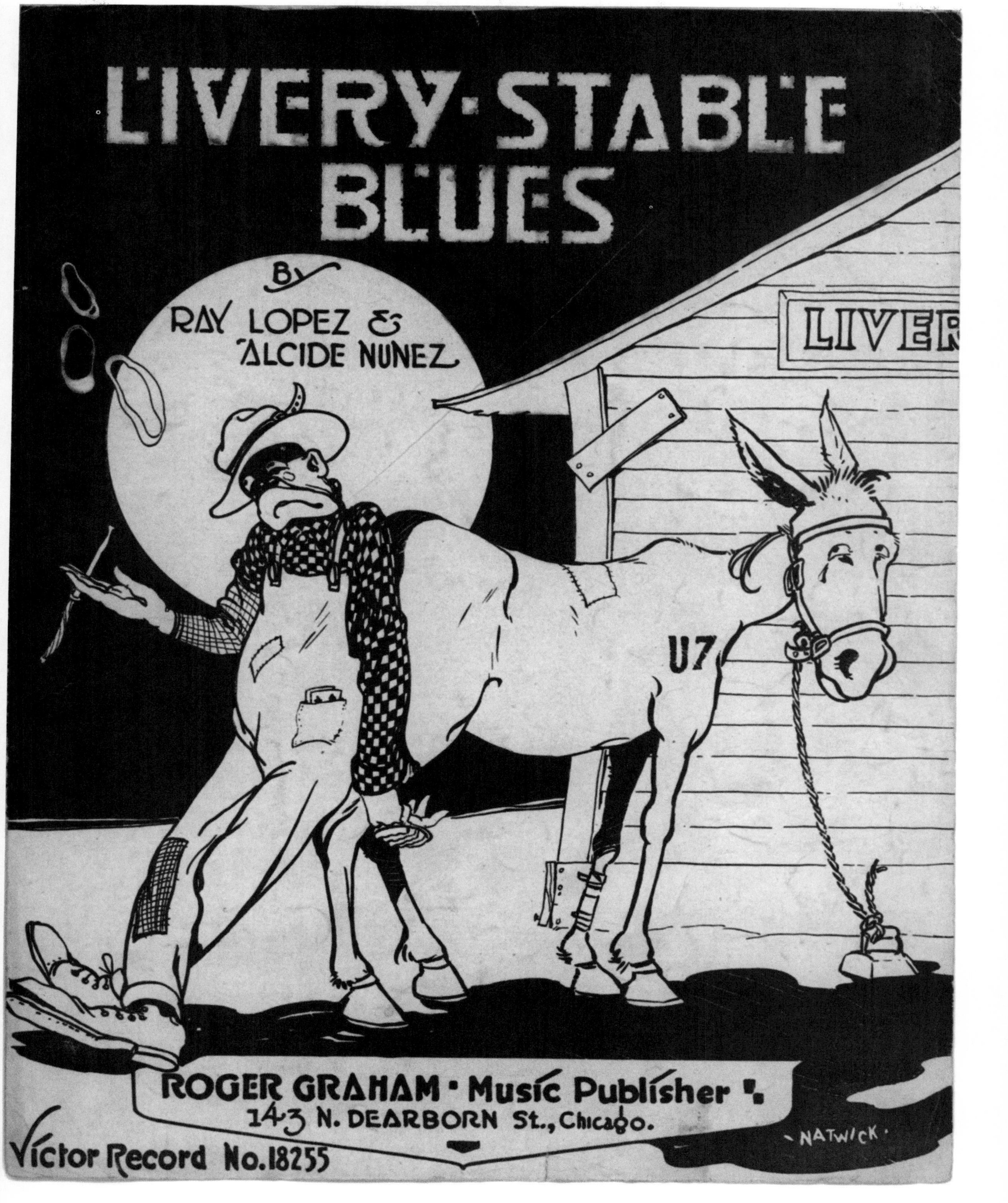
LIVERY STABLE BLUES
By
RAY LOPEZ &
ALCIDE NUNEZ
LIVER
U7
ROGER GRAHAM • Music Publisher
143 N. DEARBORN St., Chicago.
NATWICK
Victor Record No.18255

Livery Stable Blues

By RAY LOPEZ
and
ALCIDE NUNEZ
Of the Original "Dixieland Jazz Band."

Moderato.

THE LONESOME BLUES

By PERRY BRADFORD

BRADFORD & JEANETTE

PUBLISHED BY

PERRY BRADFORD

Standard Theatre,   Philadelphia, Pa.

The Lonesome Blues

Words and Music by
PERRY BRADFORD

LONG GONE

Words by
CHRIS SMITH

Music by
W. C. HANDY

76

THE MEMPHIS BLUES

Better known as
"MISTER CRUMP"

As played by
"HANDY AND HIS BAND"

Published by
THERON C. BENNETT CO.
OMAHA,   MEMPHIS,
NEW YORK,   DENVER,
149 W. 36th St.   811-16th St

The Memphis Blues
or
(Mister Crump)

By W. C. HANDY

Muscle Shoals Blues

Words and Music by
GEO. W. THOMAS
Writer of "Houston Blues"
"Oh Angel Eyes Its All For You"

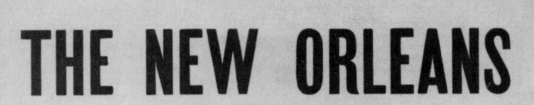

THE NEW ORLEANS

HOP. SCOP. BLUES

Words and Music

By

Geo. W. Thomas

PUBLISHED BY

GEO. W. THOMAS

MUSIC PUBLISHING HOUSE

116 S. FRANKLIN ST.,   NEW ORLEANS, LA.

The New Orleans.
Hop. Scop. Blues.

Words and Music by
GEO. W. THOMAS.

Old New Or-leans is a great big old South-ern town where hos-pi-tal-i-ty you will sure-ly find, The pop-u-la-tion there, Is ve-ry ve-ry fair, With ev'-ry thing they do they all seem to be true The blues they have down there

sure-ly is some thing rare there._____ Now lis-ten   they sound so good to you,

It will make you dance the hop scop blues   The girls in New Or-leans,

Just simp-ly are a dream,   They all are South-ern raised   You got to give them praise

They have a dance that's late, They sure are up to   date,_____

Now hon-ey, you see them col-ored Folks, go-ing to that big old Lin-coln what I mean that big old Lin-coln Park.

They dance the Hop Scop Blues, They are the best old blues, The Whi Folks dance them to, Out at the Span-ish Fort,

They ev-en dance these blues, Down on the old Sid-ney Boat_____ Right here you

Chorus. *Not fast.*

Glide, SPOKEN *Slide,* *Dance,* *Prance,* SPOKEN *Hop,*

obligato. *obligato.*

99 BLUES

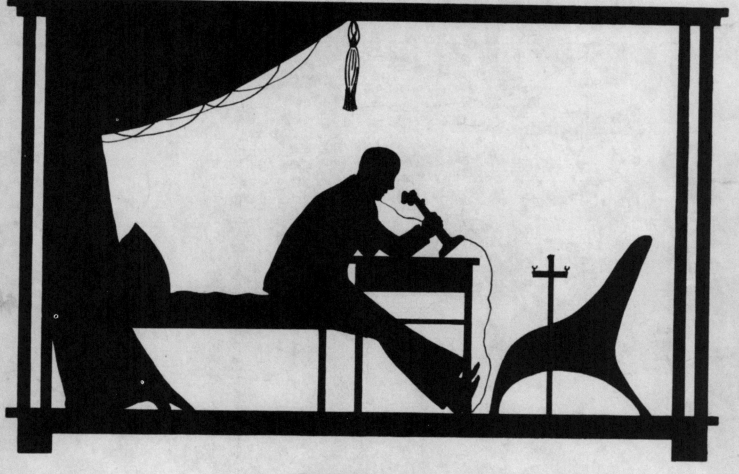

SONG

BY

GORDON SAUNDERS

AND

HENRY McCURDY

SAUNDERS MUSIC CO.
OTTAWA,   KAN.

99 BLUES

Words by
HENRY MC CURDY

Music by
S. G. SAUNDERS

The oth - er night I felt so lone - ly   I had such aw - ful
Down at the dance the oth - er eve - ning   Of course my girl was

blues ____ Then I went to the phone to try and find her a - lone   And see what she would
there ____ And she passed me by her lit - tle head held high   Just as if I would

do ____ But when I took down the re - ciev - er   The line was bus - y   still ___ I hung
care ____ But lat - er when I talked things o - ver   She said I am so   mad ___ I've

up with a bang and then went out with the gang   Sing - ing these mourn - ful   blues. ___
wait - ed all fall for a tel - e - phone call   That's why I'm feel - ing so   sad. ___

CHORUS

I've got the blues those 9 9 blues such aw-ful blues I don't know what to do But that's my

fate _____ Ev'-ry time I call that place Cent-ral says old fel-low

You've pulled a bone leave her a-lone They've on-ly got one tel-e-phone Each night I

have a fight to get the line And when I call 9 9 Hear this re-ply _____

Well if you want to talk to your sweet-ie fair You'll have to send the message thru the air

Oh boy I've got those 9 9 blues. blues. _____

OLE MISS

RAG

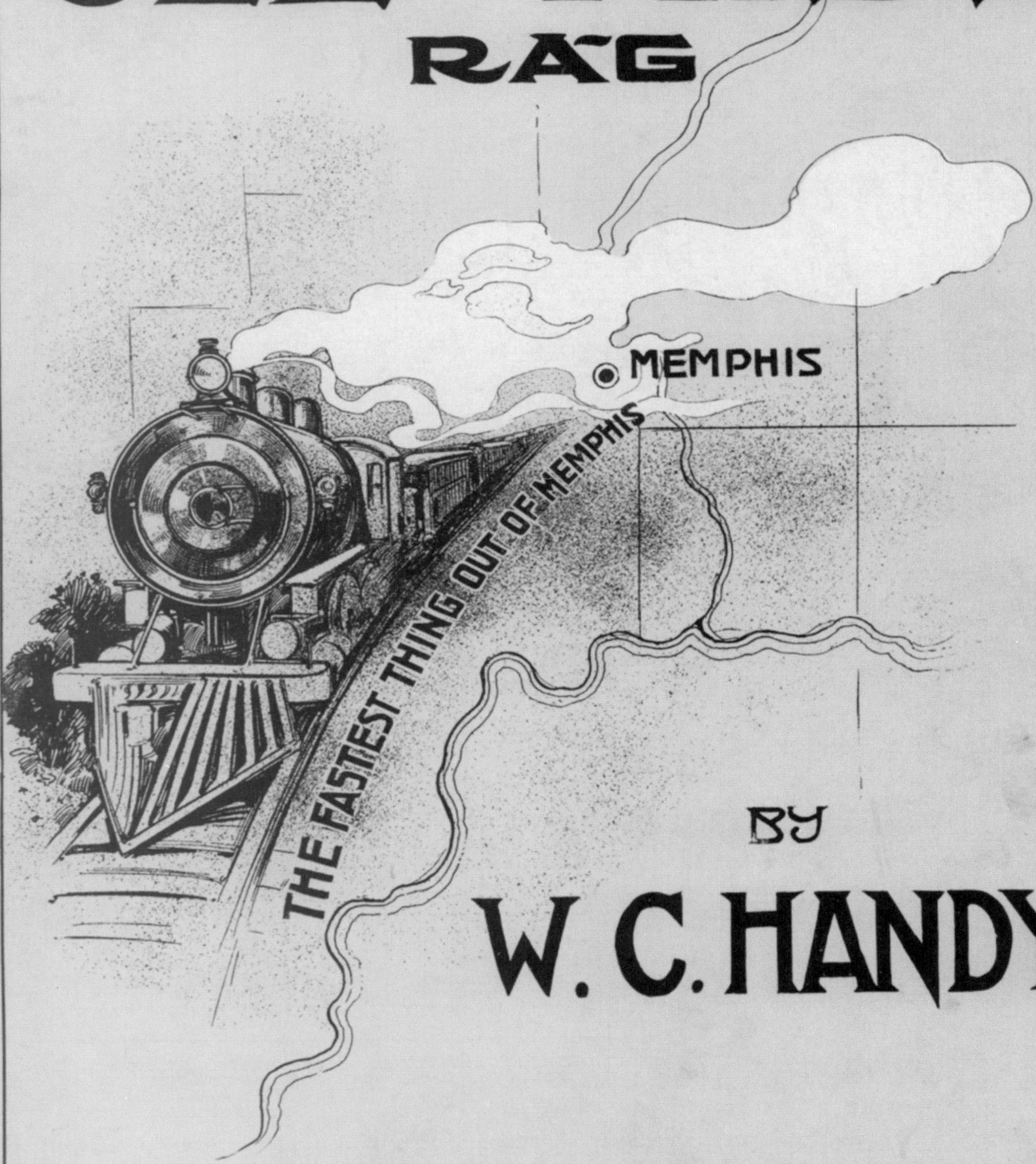

BY

W. C. HANDY

PUBLISHED BY
PACE & HANDY MUSIC CO
MEMPHIS, TENN.

5

OLE MISS
RAG

W. C. HANDY

Not too fast

A la Blues

TRIO

2ᵈ time 8ᵛᵃ

p-ff

PREPAREDNESS BLUES

by
CHAS. HILLMAN

5

Published by
PACE & HANDY MUSIC CO.
Chicago - New York.

PREPAREDNESS BLUES

CHAS. HILLMAN.

Railroad Blues

Lyric by
HAVEN GILLESPIE
and
HOWARD WASHINGTON

Music by
C. LUCKEYTH ROBERTS
Edited by Roy Bargy

102

cry - in' all the whole day through, All I want-ed was mah kiss-in; But mah
hoof it till I run him down, Tho my shoes may go to up-pers And my

ba - by is a-miss - in' once a - gain on a choo-choo train.___
up-pers go to noth-in' I'll be there, yes, I'll be there.___

En - jine whis - tles blow - in; Ding - dong Now he's go - in':

CHORUS

I've got the feel in' bad___ I've got the feel in' bad

p - f

OPERATIC EDITION
Roumania
Romance
by
Clarence Williams
Dave Peyton
Spencer Williams
60¢
WILLIAMS & PIRON
Music Publishers
177 N. State St.
CHICAGO

Roumania

By
CLARENCE WILLIAMS
DAVE PEYTON,
& SPENCER WILLIAMS

107

Wed-ding day I'm plan-ning For you

And by the star a-bove I sav-ing all my love

Rou-man-ia and it's all true blue

In dreams I........ ca-ressed you, To my heart I pressed you, You

sighed.......   Then I was.... a-waken'd   All my dreams were shaken

I........   cried........   Some-day I'll be re-turn-ing,

No more will I be yearn-ing,   For then I'll be with

you...........................   you...........................

Royal Garden Blues

Tempo di Blues

By CLARENCE WILLIAMS
and SPENCER WILLIAMS

No use of talk-in' no use of talk-in' You'll start in dog-walk-in' no mat-ter where

There's jazz-co-pa-tion blues mod-u-la-tion Just like a Hai-tian you'll rip and tear

Most ev-'ry-bo-dy likes the blues

Here's why I'm ra-vin' here's why I'm ra-vin' If it's blues you are cra-vin' just come on down

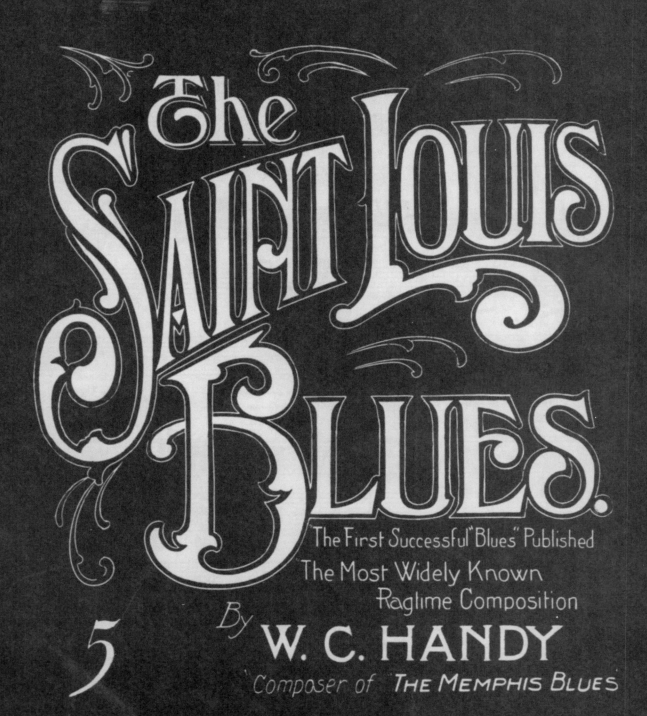

The Saint Louis Blues.

The First Successful "Blues" Published
The Most Widely Known
Ragtime Composition

By

5 W. C. HANDY

Composer of The Memphis Blues

Published by
PACE & HANDY MUSIC CO.
MEMPHIS TENN

The "St. Louis Blues"

W. C. HANDY

Moderato

Slowly

I hate to see   de eve-ning sun go   down _____   Hate to see
Been to de Gypsy   to get ma for-tune   tole _____   To de Gypsy
You ought to see   dat stove pipe brown of   mine _____   Lak he owns

de evenin' sun go   down _____   Cause ma ba - by   he done lef dis
done got ma for-tune   tole _____   Cause Im is wile   bout ma Jel-ly
de Di-mon Jo-seph   line _____   He'd make a cross-eyed   'o-man go stone

Copyright MCMXIV by W. C. Handy
Published by The Pace & Handy Music Co., Memphis, Tenn.

CHORUS
Melody from "The Jogo Blues"

Got de St Louis Blues jes blue as ah can be ___
I loves dat man lak a school-boy loves his pie ___

Dat man got a heart lak a rock cast in the sea ___
Lak a Ken-tuck-y Col'- nel loves his mint an rye, ___

Or else he would-n't gone
I'll love ma ba-by till

1. so far from me. *Spoken* Dog-gone-it!
   de day ah die.

2. me ___
   die ___

D.C.

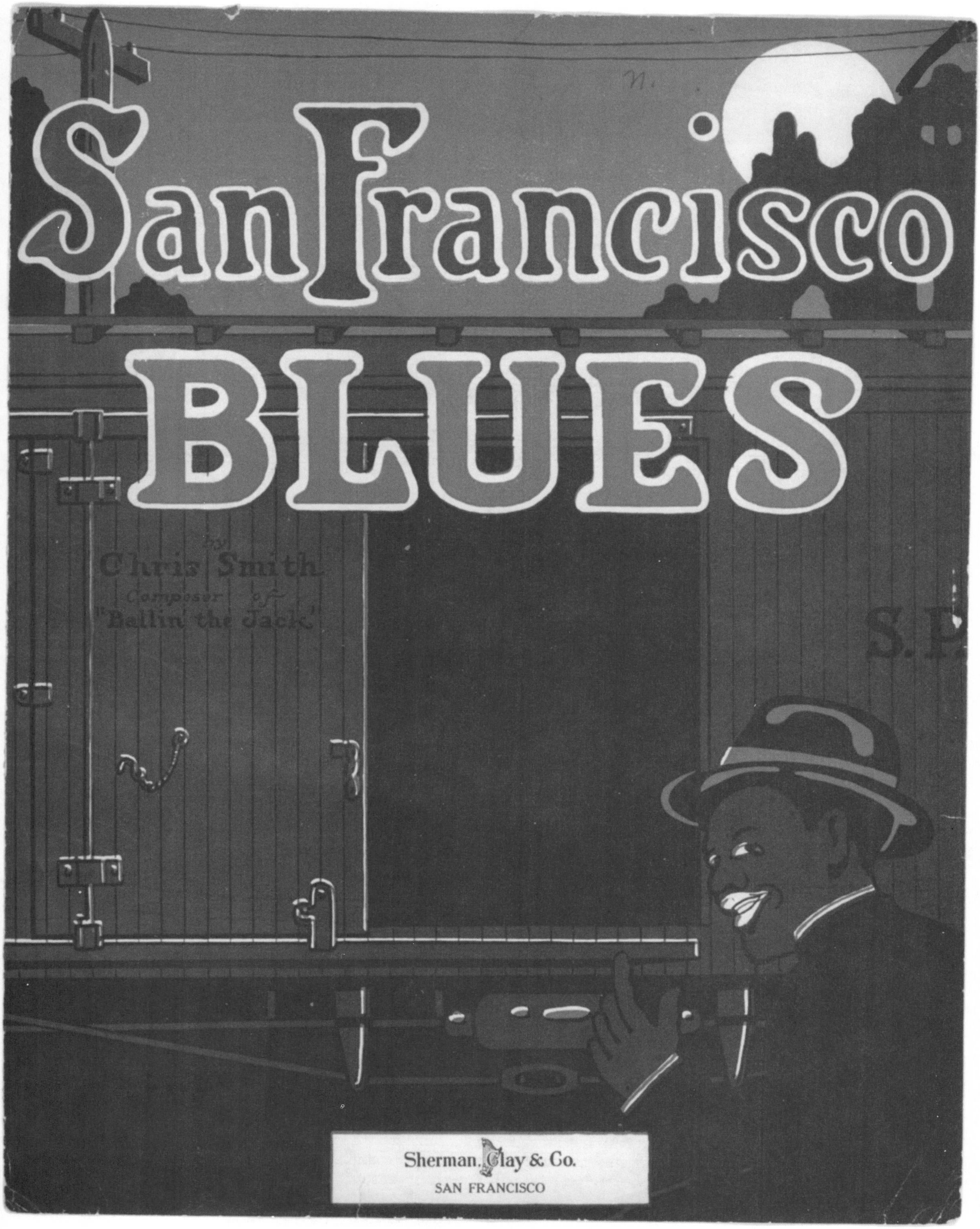
San Francisco
BLUES
by
Chris Smith
Composer of
"Ballin' the Jack."
S.P.
Sherman, Clay & Co.
SAN FRANCISCO

SAN FRANCISCO BLUES.

(FOX TROT)

By CHRIS SMITH.
Arr. by Lester E. Stevens.

Slow

"SHOEBOOT'S-SERENADE"

RAG SONG WITH TROMBONE OBLIGATO
BY
W. C. HANDY
ORIGINATOR OF THE "BLUES" STYLE IN MUSIC COMPOSITION. COMPOSER OF "THE MEMPHIS BLUES."

FEATURED
BY
TOM POST
COMEDIAN
AND
SOLOIST
WITH
J. A. COBURN'S
GREATER
MINSTRELS

PUBLISHED BY
PACE AND HANDY MUSIC CO.
MEMPHIS. TENN.

Shoeboot's Serenade

Words and Music by
W. C. HANDY

Published by Pace & Handy Music Co., Memphis,Tenn.

CHORUS
slowly

I woke up this morn - ing with the blues all 'round my bed,

Think - ing a - bout what you, my ba - by, said,

Do say the word and give my poor heart ease, The blues ain't

noth - ing but the fa - tal heart dis - ease. I'll

have to leave this town, just to wear you off my mind,

Can't sleep for dream - ing, can't laugh for cry - in',

So in the moon - - - - light Shoe-boots played ____

____ his lit-tle ser - - e - - nade. ____

rit. e dim.

SNAKEY BLUES

"An Etude In Ragtime"

By

WILL NASH.

→ 50 ←

Published by
PACE & HANDY MUSIC CO.
MEMPHIS, TENN.

The Snakey Blues

By WILL NASH

"THE BLUES" in Thirds

"FARE THEE"

Lutoso

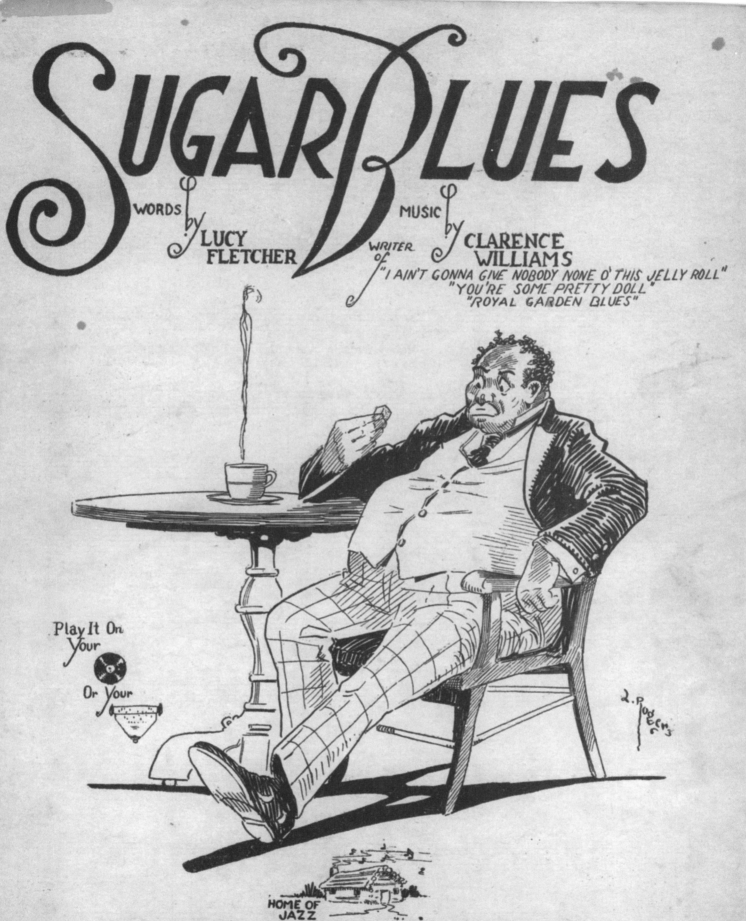

Sugar Blues

Words by
LUCY FLETCHER

Music by
CLARENCE WILLIAMS

134

CHORUS

I've got the Su_gar Blues, Every body's singing the Sugar Blues. The whole town is ringing I

love my cof_fee I love my tea But this doggone su_gar diet aint got em for me.

I'm so un hap_py, I feel so bad, I could lay me down and die. You can

say what you choose but I'm all con_fused I've got them sweet sweet su_gar blues more su_gar I've

got them sweet sweet su_gar blues   I've got the   blues.

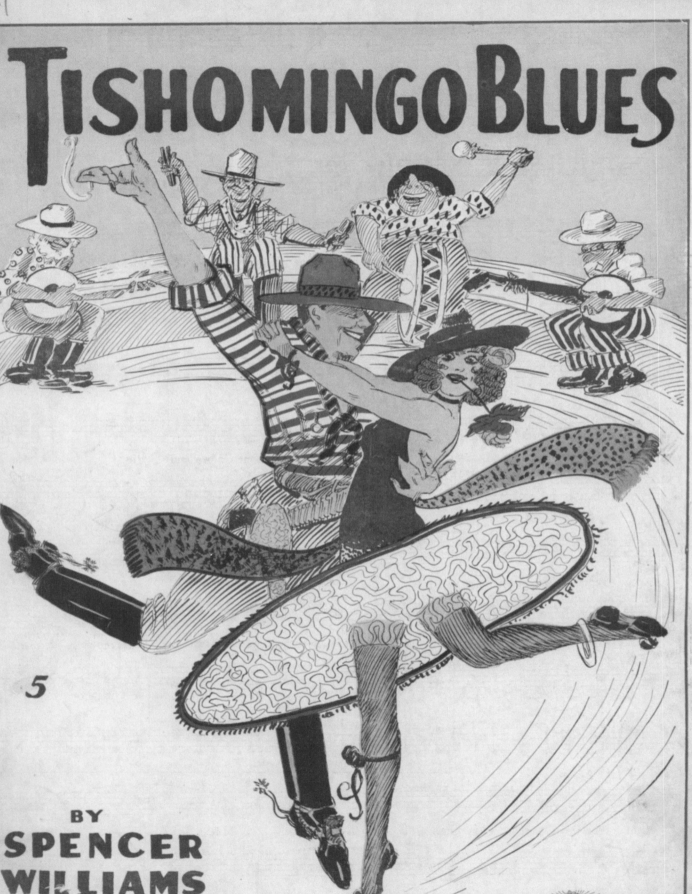

Tishomingo Blues

Words and Music by
SPENCER WILLIAMS
Writer of "Shim-me-sha-Wabble"

Oh Mis-si-sip-pi, Oh Mis-si-sip-pi, My heart cries out 'for you in sad-ness,
To-night I'm pray-in', To-night I'm say-in', Oh Lord please bless the train that takes me,

I want to be where, the win-try winds don't blow,
To Tish-o-min-go, way down old Dix-ie way,

Down where the south-ern moon swings low, That's where I want to go.
Where south-ern folks are al-ways gay, That's why you hear me say.

CHORUS

I'm goin' to Tish-o-min-go, be-cause I'm sad to-day,

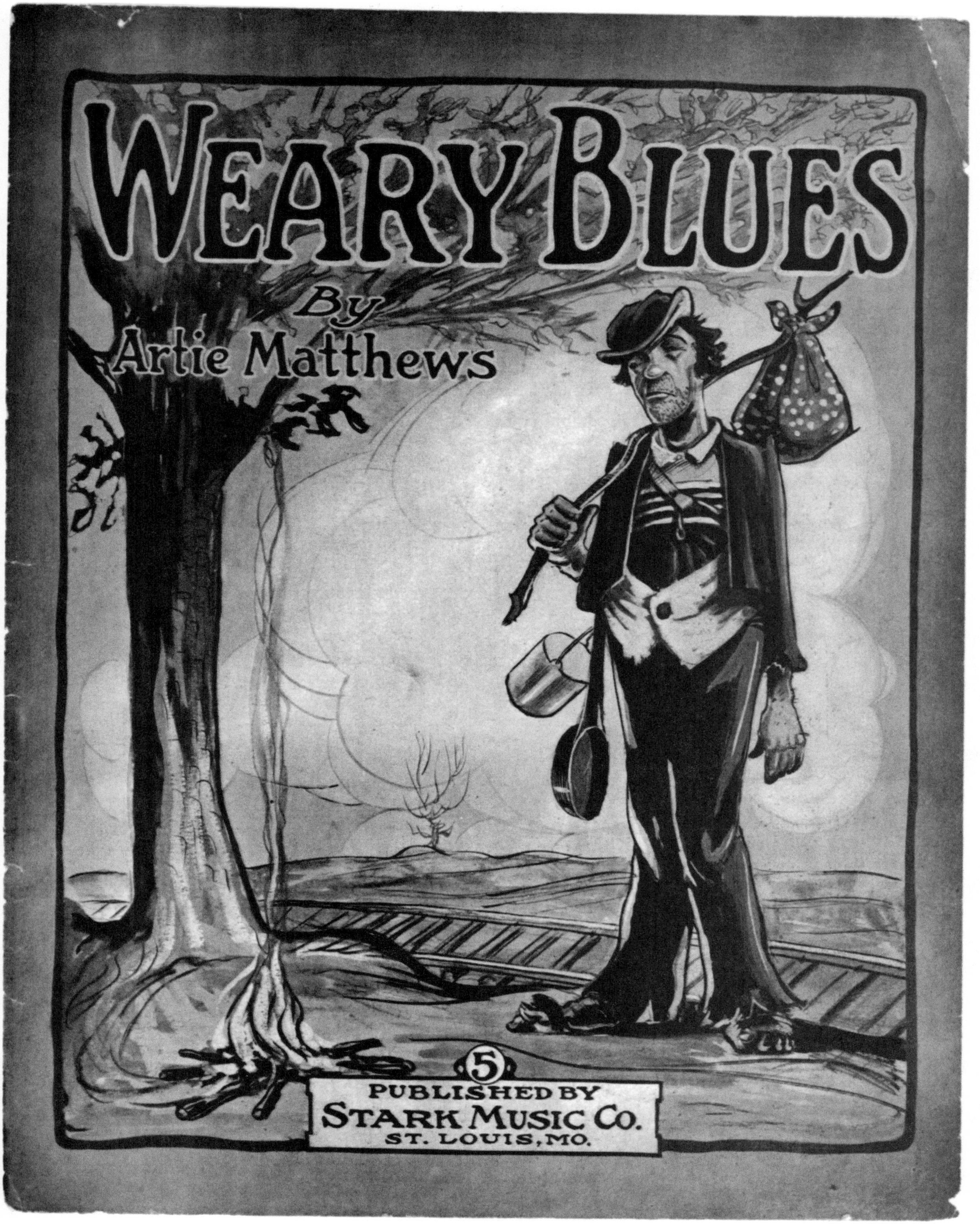
WEARY BLUES
By
Artie Matthews
5
PUBLISHED BY
STARK MUSIC CO.
ST. LOUIS, MO.

The Weary Blues

ARTIE MATTHEWS.

TRIO.

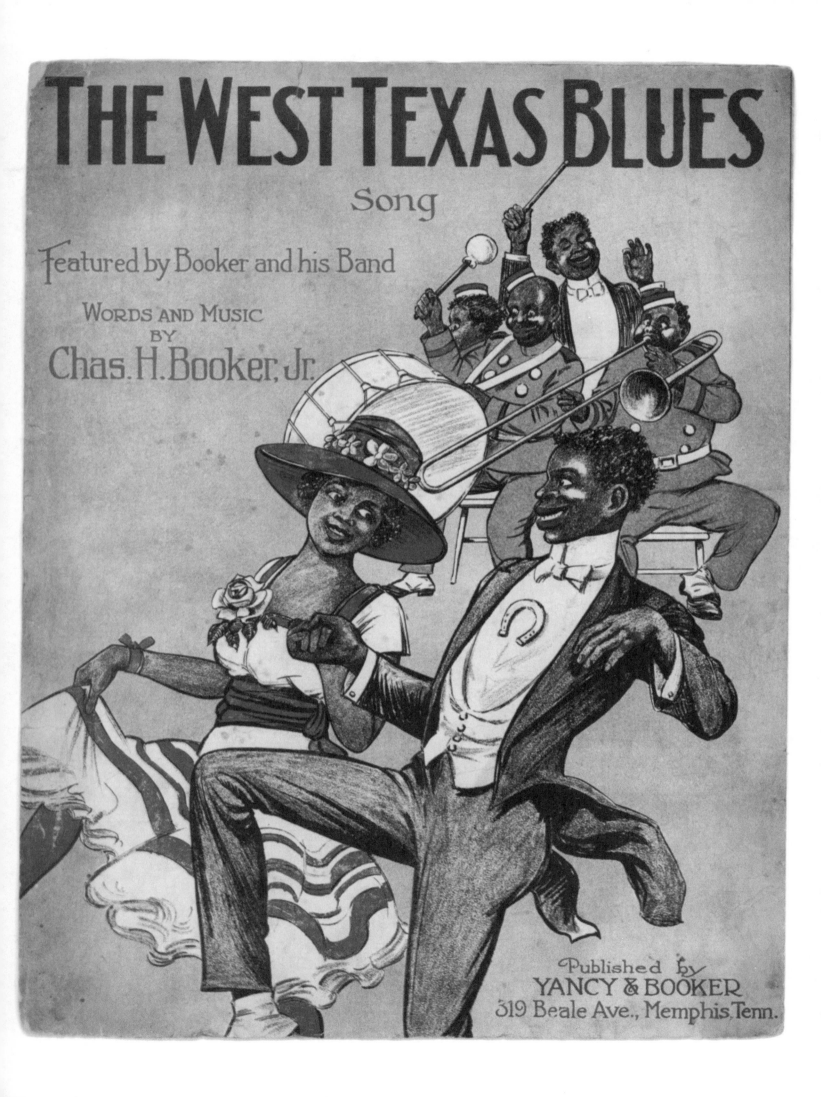

The West Texas Blues

FOX TROT

CHAS H. BOOKER, Jr.

YELLOW DOG BLUES

BY·W·C·HANDY

Joseph C. Smith · Harry Rederman

MADE·FAMOUS
BY·THE
JOSEPH·C·SMITH'S
ORCHESTRA
featuring
MR·HARRY·REDERMAN
WITH·HIS·LAUGHING
TROMBONE
VICTOR·RECORD
NO·18618

PUBLISHED BY
PACE & HANDY
MUSIC CO. INC.
(HOME OF THE BLUES)
GAIETY THEATRE BUILDING
1547 BROADWAY, NEW YORK CITY

The Yellow Dog Blues

"He's Gone Where the Southern Cross' the Yellow Dog"

W. C. HANDY